故園畫憶

庚寅中秋

韩启德题

故园画忆系列
Memory of the Old Home in Sketches

湘西风情
Folklore of Xiangxi

田明　绘画撰文
Sketches & Notes by Tian Ming

學苑出版社
Academy Press

图书在版编目（CIP）数据

湘西风情 / 田明绘、撰文．—北京:学苑出版社，2011.4

（故园画忆系列）

ISBN 978-7-5077-3760-8

Ⅰ.①湘… Ⅱ.①田… Ⅲ．①湘西土家族苗族自治州－概况 ②风俗习惯－湘西土家族苗族自治州 Ⅳ.①K926.42 ②K892.464

中国版本图书馆CIP数据核字(2011)第053637号

出 版 人：孟 白
出版发行：学苑出版社
社 址：北京市丰台区南方庄2号院1号楼
邮政编码：100079
网 址：www.book001.com
电子信箱：xueyuan@public.bta.net.cn
销售电话：010-67675512、67678944、67601101（邮购）
经 销：全国新华书店
印 刷 厂：北京信彩瑞禾印刷厂
开本尺寸：889×1194 1/24
印 张：7.25
字 数：100千字
图 幅：142幅
版 次：2011年4月北京第1版
印 次：2011年4月北京第1次印刷
定 价：36.00元

目　录

Contents

我的湘西，我的画

田　明

湘西是一块古老、秀丽和神奇的热土，历史悠久。考古发现，早在远古的石器时代，这一带就有原始人类的居住和活动。秦汉时的湘西为黔中武陵郡，三国属蜀、吴。古代统称的“五溪蛮”地，指的就是沅水中上游的雄、樠、潕、酉、辰五水流域。当然，湘西作为一个约定俗成的地域专用名称，从历史形成的地域而言，还应该包括澧水中上游以及沅水中游的一部分区域，即大湘西的概念。

湘西位于湖南省的西北部，西接云贵高原，武陵山脉由东北至西南贯穿全境，地势总体由西北向东南倾斜，碳酸盐岩广布，岩溶地貌明显。连绵数十甚至上百千米之广的崇山峻岭中有众多盆地、台地和高峰，沟谷及陡坡相互交错，山间杂树丛生，万物皆绿，一派生机。这里四季分明，“春山淡冶而笑，夏山苍翠欲滴，秋山明镜若妆，冬山惨淡如睡。”特别是位于湘西东北部的武陵源风景区，奇峰异石林立，悬崖上古木参天，由张家界国家森林公园、天子山和索溪峪自然保护区三大景区构成，被联合国教科文组织列入《世界遗产名录》，举世闻名。

湘西地处湘、鄂、渝、黔四省市交界，是古代中原与西南之间的重要通道。历史上这里是楚汉文化交界的最西端；是西南少数民族文化的最东端。从某种意义上讲，这里正是历史上西南少数民族文化与东面湘楚文化，东北部的中原文化与南端百越文化的交叉点；是长江以南沿武陵山脉直通珠江流域古文化大走廊的中部沉积处。湘西虽位于中华大地之腹地，但自古又被人们认为是“异化”之地，一直被列入“西南蛮夷”之属，十分偏远封闭。后晋天福五年所立的“溪州铜柱”，明清以来建造的湘西“苗疆边墙”，都证实了这一区域曾经是中央王朝直辖区的边界。

湘西民族风情浓郁，文化历史厚重。这里世居并生息繁衍着土家族、苗族、汉族、白族等同胞，土家族和苗族是湘西的两大主体民族，分布最广。他们用自己的勤劳勇敢和聪明才智共同创造了湘西灿烂的文化。特有的地理位置、地质特征和少数民族文化，给湘西蒙上了一层神秘的面纱。

我是一个土生土长的湘西人，是喝着猛洞河水，听着阿妈唱湘西民谣长大的。在父亲影响下一直热爱艺术，喜欢美术，方便且简单快捷的速写，就成了我感悟湘西最直接的桥梁。不需粉饰，没有做作，黑白的世界，线条的天地，随心所欲，任意涂抹。

20 世纪 80 年代初，我陪著名画家何海霞老先生到湘西采风，先后画了不少表现张家界红岩与猛洞河青岩的山水画和速写。何先生认为：湘西的山险，险中出奇；湘西的峰野，野中见方。概括起来就是四个字，险、奇、野、方，特别是最后的“方”字，道出老前辈对湘西山川的真情感受。湘西的山川，特别是那种红岩、青岩山地，断层为棱、突峰成方、群山相竞、重重叠叠，与深处之台地连成一片，气势非凡。而这种直观的感觉只要从凤凰县阿拉镇向西走去，大山从方到圆的感觉绝不是天方夜谭：前面的地势在不断上升，只见湘西这边棱角分明、参差不齐的山脉，逐渐被拉平、变大，棱角在缩小、磨平，最后融合在云贵高原的天地之间。所以，将湘西用一个“方”字来概括，真还有点道理。

方即方正厚道，方则棱角分明，但在画中如何表现，的确是个棘手的难题。开始我曾尝试借鉴西画中的透视法则，以块面辅助造型，以明暗强化棱角，其样子虽方了，但总感到缺点什么。我曾学于南京，深造在北京，金陵画派和北方山水对我影响都较大。我努力揣摩荆浩、范宽及龚贤、黄宾虹等老前辈的风格传统，将表现江南山峦润泽的意境与北国山川雄浑苍凉的气魄的手法结合，加上自己在湘西生活几十年的体验。中法为本，西法为用。曾经也有人问我：你的画属文人还是院体？你的速写是素材的收集，还是对景的创作？我懵了，这一点的确还没有认真想过。想怎么画就怎么画，完全是跟着感觉走。我常常将构图安排得很满，使画面有一种向外的张力，在一尊尊向上的群峰中间，大面积的用倾斜线穿叉出层层大山、台地及断层。在树木房舍上大胆地进行变形归纳，甚至有些装饰性的图案化倾向，以求与线条造型的整体协调。最后在吊脚楼旁添几头黄牛、点几个苗女壮汉，在绿水溪流和蓝天之中加一叶扁舟、飞一行翠鸟白鹭。着意刻画出一番浓浓的湘西地域风情。

画得好不好也许并不重要，重要的是有没有湘西的味道。仁者见仁，智者见智。希望我的画像武陵山上的老酒包谷烧 ，醇香劲足；似湘西人家的老腊肉，美味地道。细细品来，归成一个“土”字，凝为一个“情”字。“土”的自然，“情”的质朴。只要是真诚的，真正走进湘西，走进湘西人的心里，用湘西人特有的眼光看待这些曾养育过世代湘西人的山川，用湘西人的情感去体验这些曾浸透湘西人血汗的大地。“诗言志”、“画言情”，诗情画意，博大精深，这才是有血有肉的湘西，我心中的湘西！

我始终记得我的朋友和老师、南京书画院朱道平院长对我的勉励：“田明的画，来自大山之中，充满大山的气息。郁郁的山林和苍崖，在画面中是那样贴近和真切地抚慰着观者的心，也不禁使我回想起数年前我首来大庸（张家界）感受到的一切。湘西的山川是壮美的，生活在这里的画家是幸运的，因为他可以朝夕面对大山的云起云飞、朝晖夕阴，实则画家如没有对生活的真切体验，画面将会是苍白的。田明是很努力的，当然他也面对许多苦恼的问题，他冀求在作品的感情、意境等高层次上寻求新的突破，他始终感到不满足，我相信他会越画越好的，我们祝愿他更上一层楼。”

“路漫漫其修远兮，吾将上下而求索”。湘西的山水是美丽的，湘西的人文是丰厚的，湘西的自然是生态的。冒昧地拿出这些年来我眼中的湘西，一个心灵的寄托，一份羞涩的答卷。探索仅仅只是开始，今后的路会更长、更长！

My Xiangxi, My sketching

Tian Ming

Xiangxi, the northwestern part of Hu'nan Province neighbors the Yunnan–Guizhou Plateau to the west. The Wuling Mountains zigzag through the Prefecture, with the topography inclining from northwest to southeast. This part of the world features karst landforms, with peculiar peaks, grotesque rocks, rivers and caves. The Wulingyuan Scenic and Historic Interest Area in northeast Xiangxi has been listed as a World Heritage site by the UNESCO. It is composed of the National Forest Park of Zhangjiajie, the Tianzishan Mountain and the Suoxiyu Nature Reserves.

Xiangxi has a long history and boasts picturesque landscape. Archeological findings show that people lived here as early as in the Stone Age. Xiangxi was the location of Wuling County in the Qin (221 BC–206 BC) and Han (202 BC–220 AD) Dynasties; during the period of the Three Kingdoms (220–280 A.D.), it was under the jurisdiction of the Shu State and the Wu State. In ancient times the region was known as "Wuximan" ("five rivers tribes folks"), – the area drained by the Xionghe, Manhe, Wushui, Youhe and Chenhe Rivers in the middle and upper reaches of the Yuanshui River. Of course, Xiangxi, as the name of a region, historically included the areas in the middle and upper reaches of the Lishui River, a Greater Xiangxi.

Xiangxi sits at the place where Hu'nan, Hubei and Guizhou Provinces and Chongqing Municipality meet. It served as an important passageway between the Central Plains and southwestern China in ancient times. Historically it was a meeting point of minority culture in southwest China, Xiang–Chu culture to the east, Central Plains culture to northeast and Bai–Yue culture to the south.

With colorful ethnic customs, a long history and a rich culture, Xiangxi is home to the Tujia, Miao, Han, Bai and other ethnic groups. They lived in harmony and worked hard to create the splendid Xiangxi culture with their own industry, bravery, wisdom and intelligence. The ancient town of Wangcun, the border town of Chadong, the Qin Dynasty (221BC–206 BC) town of Liye, and ancient city of Fenghuang, like bright pearls shining in the emerald mountains, are places for people to escape the bustle and mundane affairs of modern cities and gain inner calm. They can also see thrilling performance here, such as "Climbing the Sword Ladder", "Going down to the Sea of Fire", and the "Maogusi dance" or "Hand–waving Dance". Such colorful folk customs, distinct geographical location, geological characteristics and ethnic minority culture combine to make Xiangxi somewhat mysterious.

Mountains in Xiangxi include those with red rock or blue rock; faults are angular and peaks are regular. Lofty and precipitous peaks, joining together with mesa to give strong impression to people here. Mr. He Haixia, a famous Chinese painter, describes Xiangxi in this way: The mountains in Xiangxi are precipitous and peculiar, and the peaks there are unbelievably wild and upright. He sums up what he said with four words: "precipitous", "peculiar", "wild" and "regular". The word "regular" expresses Mr. He's true feeling about the mountains in Xiangxi.

I was born and brought up in Xiangxi. When I was young, I drank water from the Mengdonghe River and listened to stories told by Mom, who also sang folk songs of Xiangxi for me. My father was an artist. Under his influence, I have loved art, especially the fine arts, since young. In the long years of work, I have created many sketches of Xiangxi, and, from this, I gained a better understanding of the region, my hometown.

In the face of the strange environment, how to show the "regular" of mountains in Xiangxi in sketches is really a hard nut to crack. In the beginning, I tried to do this by borrowing the western techniques of perspective. Blocks were created and dark and bright colors were applied to show edges and corners. The sketches looked "regular", but I often thought it lacked something to be really regular. Later, when I made further study of the style and tradition of the Jinling Painting School and Northern Landscape Painting School of traditional Chinese painting, I learned to combine the way the lush green mountains of the south are portrayed with the way the magnificent mountains in north China are painted. This, plus dozens of years of experience in creative work, made it possible for me to paint according to true feelings and needs. All these are aimed at depicting the customs and habits of Xiangxi.

Whether the paintings I have created are good or not is not important. What is important is whether I have brought out a real Xiangxi in the work.

吉首

Jishou

吉首系苗语，意为“地大繁荣而地位重要”。明洪武三十年（1397）在此设千户所，曾名“所里”。1949 年，依苗语音译改称吉首。现为湘西土家族苗族自治州首府，是湘西黄金旅游的集散中心。

苗族历史悠久，分支众多，湘西苗族自称“果雄”，是蚩尤三苗之后裔，远古时期长途迁徙定居于此。湘西苗族刚毅骁勇，勤劳热情，以自己的智慧融合本土文明，创造了独具一格的湘西苗族文化。

Founded in 1397, Jishou is now the capital of Tujia Miao Autonomous Prefecture in western Hu'nan Province (Xiangxi).

The Miao people have a long history and many branches. In Xiangxi, they refered to themselves Guo Xiong. Having settled here in ancient times, they merged their own wisdom with the locdl culture and created their own unique Miao culture in Xiangxi.

2008 年

苗家女

（吉首）

湘西苗族群属较多，从服饰上有腊尔山、社塘坡、丹青和保靖、花垣之不同，各有千秋，异彩分呈。

Miao Woman

Location: Jishou

The Miao people in Xiangxi are of many different sub-groups, each of which can be recognized by their unique dress style.

峒河半边街

（吉首　峒河）

峒河边的一条老街，一边是河水，一边是商铺。

Tonghe one-side street

Location: Donghe River, Jishou
With the river flowing along one side of the street, shops line the other side.

2004 年

东门拉拉渡

（吉首　峒河）

拉拉渡是仅依靠一根连接两岸的绳索牵引船来往的摆渡方式。不用桨楫风帆，一根绳索就串起峒河两岸的千年风霜。

Dongmen Cable Ferry

Location: Donghe River, Jishou
Instead of oars or a sail, a piece of rope has served as the link across the river for thousands of years.

1992 年

巴代作法

（吉首　社塘坡）

“巴代”是苗家的巫师，为本地德高望众的能人。主持还愿请神、消灾避难等活动。

Badai Shamans

Location: Shetangpo, Jishou

The Miao people call their shaman Badai. A Badai is practicing his craft.

2006 年

2007年

女舞狮手

(吉首　社塘坡)

苗家狮舞辟邪纳吉，十分讲究。舞狮人技艺过人，为大家所敬重。女舞狮人英姿飒爽，光彩照人。

Female Lion Dancers

Location: Shetangpo, Jishou
Female dancers performing the traditional Chinese lion dance can rarely be seen except among the Miao folk.

胡家塘

（吉首　乾州）

胡家塘是一个始建于明朝的长条形人造池塘。这一带还有石桥、古井和一些古建筑，体现着明清及民国时期建筑的风貌特点。

Hujiatang

Location: Qianzhou, Jishou
Buildings on this historic street are in the Ming (1368—1644) and Qing (1644—1911) dynasty styles.

2001 年

2005年

乾州老码头

（吉首　乾州）

乾州是一座石头垒成的古城，旧时有“乾州”而无“吉首”。宋熙宁三年（1070）即置镇溪砦，清康熙四十三年（1704）设乾州厅。乾州是“中国南方长城”军事防御体系的指挥中心之一。1953年，随着各行政机构迁至今吉首市区，喧闹了数百年的乾州古城渐渐淡出了人们的视线。万溶江傍城而过，江边的老码头曾经是进出乾州的重要关口。城内建筑古色古香，汉文化、楚巫文化与湘西少数民族文化积淀丰厚。

Old Wharf in Qianzhou

Location: Qianzhou, Jishou

Qianzhou is an ancient town which was part of "the southern great wall of China". The old wharf by the river Wanrongjiang used to be an important pass in and out of Qianzhou .

湘川公路奇观

（吉首　矮寨）

1935 年建成，是一段在悬崖上开凿的公路，人称“矮寨天险”，为湘川公路上最险的关卡。此处有中国的第一座公路立交桥。

The Marvelous Xiang-Chuan Highway

Location: Aizhai, Jishou

Built in 1935, this is the most dangerous mountain pass of Xiang-Chuan Highway linking Hu'nan with Sichuan. Here you may find china's first highway overpass.

2008 年

2008 年

矮寨苗家

（吉首　矮寨）

矮寨是一个苗族聚居地，距吉首 20 千米，位于一峡谷口，地势险峻。矮寨民居几乎全用天然青石板建造，墙、屋顶和晒谷场均用平整的天然石板垒拼而成。

Aizhai Village

Location: Aizhai, Jishou

It is a settlement totally occupied by the Miao people. Houses in Aizhai village are built almost solely with slate or black-stone.

矮寨后山

（吉首　矮寨）

矮寨后山的山势跌宕，绝壁高耸，悬崖与山谷梯田相映衬。

Aizhai Back Mountain

Location: Aizhai, Jishou

Stunning views of the cliffy peaks of the mountain.

1999 年

苗族鼓手

（吉首　矮寨）

矮寨是有名的苗族鼓舞之乡。苗族鼓舞又称“跳鼓”，苗语为“雀龙”，分布很广，各具特色，是苗家喜闻乐见的一种风俗，也是喜庆娱乐必不可少的民族传统项目。

Miao Drummers

Location: Aizhai, Jishou
The Drum Dance is a popular traditional performance seen in many celebrations of the Miao people.

2006年

母子情深

（吉首　矮寨）

母爱是世界上最伟大的情感，有妈的孩子像个宝。一对苗族母子情深意浓的写真。

Mother and Son

Location: Aizhai, Jishou
Mother's love, the greatest love of all.

2007 年

德夯苗寨

（吉首　矮寨）

德夯，苗语为“美丽的峡谷”之意。位于吉首西郊 24 千米处。秀美的山涧水色与独特的苗家风情融为一体，为湖南省十大重点旅游区之一。德夯苗寨的民居是清一色的青瓦木板屋，纵横交错的青石板路串连着百余户人家。九龙溪穿寨而过，一座古朴典雅的石拱桥横跨山溪。

Dehangmiao Village

Location: Aizhai, Jishou

Dehang, means beautiful canyon in Miao language. The village features wooden houses with gray -tiled roofs and criss-cross gray stone roads.

2007 年

三姊妹峰

（吉首　矮寨）

德夯新寨背后山梁上有三座形似穿着花罗裙苗族少女的灰白色石峰。

Three Sisters Peak

Location: Aizhai, Jishou
Three greyish-white rocky peaks look like three Miao girls dressed in floral skirts.

1996 年

孔雀开屏

（吉首　矮寨）

德夯九龙溪边上，有一座形似孔雀开屏的山峰。

A Peacock Displaying its Plumage

Location: Aizhai, Jishou

The mountains resemble a peacock showing off its tail plumage.

1996 年

问天台

（吉首 矮寨）

德夯玉泉溪景区内，一座四周群山环绕，山顶为平台的独立小山头。

Wentian Platform

Location: Aizhai, Jishou
A single hill with a flat top.

2009 年

苗家拦门

（吉首　矮寨）

拦门是好客的苗家迎接贵客的传统仪式。每当贵客来临，一幅花带苗绣横路挡于寨门之外，乡亲们吹打弹唱，姑娘们盛装对歌敬酒，十分风趣热闹。

The Lanmen Ritual

Location: Aizhai, Jishou

Lanmen is a ritual of the Miao people when welcoming guests to their village. The literally meaning of the word is "blocking the gate".

2006 年

双龙风光

（吉首　矮寨）

双龙民俗风光大峡谷由大龙洞和小龙洞瀑布群及周边苗家民俗风光带组成，距吉首 40 千米。奇峰飞瀑、河湾筒车、苗家民居、云雾炊烟随四季而变幻，田园风光如人间仙境。

Shuanglong Scene

Location: Aizhai, Jishou

Miao settlements nestle in this vast valley surrounded by groups of water falls.

2008 年

大兴寨（一）

（吉首　矮寨）

峒河上游的一座古老苗家村寨墟场。

Daxing Village (1)

Location: Aizhai, Jishou

An ancient Miao village marketplace in the upper reaches of the Dong River.

2009 年

大兴寨（二）

（吉首　矮寨）

峒河上游的一座古老苗家村寨墟场。

Daxing Village (2)

Location: Aizhai, Jishou
An ancient Miao village marketplace in the upper reaches of the Dong River.

2009 年

2006 年

龙洞人家

（吉首　矮寨）

石板路、吊脚楼掩映在峡谷山水之间。

Life in Longdong

Location: Aizhai, Jishou
The houses and stone roads in a Miao village.

1993 年

巴夭村口

（吉首　丹青）

丹青有吉首的“西伯利亚”之称，交通不便，民风奇特，是一块被遗忘的文化宝地。这里生活着湘西苗族的一个分支——仡佬苗。巴夭村是仡佬苗生活的一个村寨。

The Entrance of Bayao Village

Location: Danqing, Jishou

Bayao village is a remote Gelao Miao village, with unique customs.

丹青仡佬苗

（吉首　丹青）

仡佬苗是湘西苗族的一个分支，可能是本地古老土著与三苗融合的后裔，也有“瓦乡人”之称。其服饰、风俗、语言都与周边的其他苗族有许多不同，鲜为人知。

Danqing Gelao-Miao

Location: Danqing, Jishou
Gelao-Miao is one of the branches of Xiangxi Miao. The people are also called "Waxiang Folk".

2006 年

太平司马村

（吉首　太平）

太平司马村位于吉首西部风光秀丽的司马河畔。这里是中国国画大师、中国画马“四杰”之一的张一尊先生的故乡。

Taiping Sima Village

Location: Taiping, Jishou
A historic village alongside the scenic Sima River.

1993 年

司马河畔的民居

（吉首　太平）

据传明代一位官居司马的朝廷大员曾来到此地，其后此溪流便名为司马河。河畔民居保留着古朴传统。

Houses along the Banks of Sima River

Location: Taiping, Jishou
The houses on stilts alongside Sima River.

1993 年

凤凰

Fenghuang

凤凰是国家历史文化名城，也是"中国最美丽的小城"之一，位于吉首市西南。始建于清康熙三十九年（1700），至今已有300多年的历史。它犹如一幅古老的山水画长卷，虽历经沧桑仍保存完整，城池巍峨，沱江悠悠，深巷老宅，古风犹存。它孕育了一代文豪沈从文、大师画家黄永玉等名流宗师。它像一壶苗疆老酒，醇香味浓，让人慢慢品尝……

Fenghuang ("phoenix") is an ancient town with a history of more than 300 years (first built in 1700) and is on the list of Historical and Cultural Cities of China.

北门城楼

（凤凰　沱江）

凤凰古城标志性建筑之一。

The North-Gate Tower

Location: Tuojiang, Fenghuang

One of the landmarks of the historic Fenghuang City.

2006 年

关门码头

（凤凰　沱江）

这里曾经是古代凤凰城的城防要塞。

Guanmen Wharf

Location: Tuojiang, Fenghuang
This used to be a fortification of the ancient Fenghuang Town.

1989 年

古街小巷

（凤凰　沱江）

石板路、石板桥、吊脚楼，是凤凰的典型街景风貌。

Lanes in the Old Town

Location: Tuojiang, Fenghuang
Stone pavements, stone bridges, houses on stilts are typical scenes of Fenhuang.

2005 年

水门码头

（凤凰　沱江）

码头，古城人走向世界的地方。

Shuimen Wharf

Location: Tuojiang, Fenghuang
This is where the local people start their journey to the outside world.

2007 年

2005 年

沱江人家

（凤凰　沱江）

凤凰古城特有的吊脚楼群，支撑了百余年的沧桑岁月。

Homes on Tuojiang River

Location: Tuojiang, Fenghuang
Homes on Tuojiang River: Such houses on stilts can only be found in the old Fenghuang Town.

两个喷呐客

（凤凰　沱江）

响亮高昂的唢呐是动听的民间器乐，每逢喜庆婚嫁，唢呐客不请自到，必不可少。

Two Suona Players

Location: Tuojiang, Fenghuang

Suona is a traditional Chinese musical instrument. Suona players would not miss any occasion to celebrate.

2008 年

全胜营南长城遗址

(凤凰　廖家桥)

全胜营南长城遗址是中国南方长城的一个重要关隘，也是中国南方长城目前保存最完好的一段。中国南方长城即“苗疆边墙”，始筑于明代万历四十三年（1615），竣工于明天启二年（1622），南起与贵州交界的亭子关，北至保靖县的涂乍，长约200千米。它是明清王朝为控制当地苗民而修建的军事设施，记录着一段血雨腥风的悲苦往事。

Quanshengying Site of the South Great Wall of China

Location: Liaojiaqiao, Fenghuang

The South Great Wall of China is about 200 kilometers long, built between 1615 and 1622 A. D. This part of the south great wall is the most well-preserved.

2008 年

黄丝桥古城东门——和育门

（凤凰　阿拉）

黄丝桥古城是我国现存最完好的石头城堡之一，距凤凰县城 26 千米。始建于唐垂拱二年 (686)，原为渭阳县治，后成为千里苗疆边墙线上最大屯兵要地。

East Gate of Huangsiqiao Historic Town

Location: Ala, Fenghuang
The Huangsiqiao ancient town is a stone fort first built in 686 A.D. in Tang Dynasty (618-907 A. D.)

2008 年

三潭书院主楼

（凤凰　吉信）

三潭书院是湘西最古老的书院之一，坐落在凤凰吉信。始建于清同治十一年 (1873)，培养了一批又一批杰出人才。

Main Building of Santan Academy

Location: Jixin, Fenghuang
Santan Academy is an academy first built in 1873.

2009 年

1995 年

得胜营内老建筑

（凤凰　吉信）

得胜营又名吉信，是苗疆边墙上的几大兵营驻地之一。

Old Buildings in Deshengying

Location: Jixin, Fenghuang

Deshengying is an ancient barracks along the Miaojiang walls.

2006 年

苗乡新事

（凤凰　吉信）

苗族同胞如今已融入现代社会，不再封闭，手机通讯也成为苗家人必不可少的交流方式。

Modern Miao People

Location: Jixin, Fenghuang
A Miao Woman Using a Mobile Phone.

2002 年

山江苗王老寨

(凤凰　山江)

山江是解放前湘西苗王龙云飞（1885—1950）的故里，也是苗族聚居之腹地。这里有最为地道的苗家风情，到处都是由自然天成的石板建造的苗家石寨。中国苗族民俗博物馆坐落于此。

The Old House of the King of Miao

Location: Shanjiang, Fenghuang
The old house of the king of Miao, Long Yunfei (1885-1950 A.D.) in Xiangxi. Now it serves as the Miao Folklore Museum.

苗家吊脚楼

(凤凰　麻冲)

苗家吊脚楼的下部用条石和土砖围砌，以为防盗。

Miao Houses on Stilts

Location: Machong, Fenghuang

The lower part of the houses are bricked with long stones and clay bricks to prevent burglary.

1999年8月14日

麻冲苗寨

（凤凰　麻冲）

麻冲苗寨依山而建，青瓦青石黄土砖砌就的民居，青石板铺就的小路，林木掩映，如诗如画。

Machong Miao Village

Location: Machong, Fenghuang
The village was built against the mountain with black tiles, black-stone and yellow clay and the roads were paved with black stones.

2002 年 9 月 1 日

腊尔山

（凤凰　腊尔山）

腊尔山是湘西的高寒台地，明清时称为“生苗”聚居区，是湘西苗族繁衍生息之地。

La’er Mountain

Location: La’ershan, Fenghuang
La’er Mountain is a high plateau where Xiangxi Miao live and thrive.

1999 年 8 月 14 日

苗族大娘

（凤凰　麻冲）

苗族妇女并不因为终日劳作就忘记自己是个女人，爱美天性依然保存。胸口前和裤脚边的扣花装饰，是劳动之余在茶油灯光下做成的。“刺绣是苗族女人的基本手艺，她们用斑斓的彩线和灵巧的针法，在自己的衣服上记载了祖先的苦难历史。”（沈从文语）

An Old Miao

Location: Machong, Fenghuang
Embroidery is a skill every Miao woman must master.

2003 年

乌巢河下苗寨

（凤凰　腊尔山）

乌巢河位于苗疆腹地腊尔山下，至今鲜为人知。下苗寨是一座依山而建的古老苗寨，亦称旱苗寨。其纯朴的民风，俨然就是一座天然的苗家博物馆。

Lower Miao Village at Wuchao River

Location: La'ershan, Fenghuang
The Wuchao river is at the foot of La'er Mountain and the village was built against the mountain.

1999 年

乌巢河上苗寨

（凤凰　腊尔山）

上苗寨依水而建，亦称水苗寨。其历经了多少次暴雨山洪的洗礼，岿然不动，的确有几分神奇。

Upper Miao Village at Wuchao River

Location: La'ershan, Fenghuang
The Maio village is built alongside the river.

1999 年

天下第一石拱桥

（凤凰　腊尔山）

第一石拱桥又名乌巢河大桥，建成于 1990 年，位于凤凰腊尔山乌巢河峡谷处。大桥长 236 米，宽 8 米，高 42 米，势若巨龙腾空，气壮山河。其单孔跨径 120 米，为世界之最。大桥采用巧妙的全空石肋拱式结构，青灰色白云岩为石料，工艺精细，体态美观，乃巧夺天工。

The Number-One Arched Stone Bridge Under Heaven

Location: La'ershan, Fenghuang

It was finished in 1990. The bridge is also named Wuchaohe Bridge since it is built upon the Wuchaohe Canyon in La'er Mountain. The main span of the bridge is 120 meters, a world record.

1999 年

腊尔山下苗寨

（凤凰　腊尔山）

腊尔山区是湘西苗族的核心聚居区，民风淳朴，有苗族自然博物馆之誉。土砖和条石砌就的籽登屋是腊尔山区苗寨的典型民居。

Lower Miao Village at La'er Mountain

Location: La'ershan, Fenghuang

La'er Mountain area is where the Miao people live in a compact community. Buildings with clay bricks and long stones are typical of the houses in La'er mountain areas. It is called "zi-deng" house.

1999 年

2006 年

晨妆

（凤凰　禾库）

湘西苗家妇女有缠长头帕的传统习俗，特别是凤凰的苗家女，其头帕长者达一丈五尺有余，每天早晨梳妆打扮，包头帕必不可少。

Morning Dress

Location: Heku, Fenghuang

The Miao women wrap their hair with a piece of scarf as long as 5 meters.

永顺 Yongshun

古溪州所在地。清雍正七年（1729）置永顺县，治所在今灵溪镇。曾为湘西北土家族政治、文化、经济的中心，自然、人文风光种类丰富。20世纪六七十年代是全国各美术院校来湘西教学或写生的首选地之一。

In 1729, the county of Youngshun was established. Yongshun, where ancient Xizhou was, used to be the political, cultural and economic center of northern Tujia folk in Xiangxi. It boasts a variety of natural resources and cultural heritage.

1988 年

灵溪镇东门桥头

（永顺　灵溪）

灵溪镇东门的一座廊桥。吊脚楼立于河岸崖壁上，人们过往休憩于廊桥。

East Gate Bridge in Lingxi Town.

Location: Lingxi, Yongshun

A covered bridge at the east gate of Lingxi Town. Houses on stilts perch on the cliff along the river. People relax in the roofed bridge.

梯子岩

（永顺　灵溪）

山崖夹峙中的梯子岩古栈道曾是连接湖北、四川地区与常德、长沙的官道，可以说是湘西的“茶马古道”。

Ladder Rock

Location: Lingxi, Yongshun

A part of the ancient road on the cliff. It used to be a place connecting Hubei, Sichuan, Changde and Changsha of Hu'nan, etc.

2001 年

小甘溪古驿道

（永顺　首车）

穿行在土家山寨小甘溪的古道，曾连接着山里和山外，滋养着那个久逝的岁月。

The Xiaoganxi Ancient Post Road

Location: Shouche, Yongshun

The ancient road zigzagging among the villages of Tujia people, linking the mountainous area and outside.

2004 年

泽家湖土家转角楼群

（永顺　泽家）

武陵山区最典型的土家族民居建筑群。

A Group of Tujia Galleried Buildings at Zejiahu

Location: Zejia, Yongshun

A most typical Tujia dwelling in Wulingshan area.

2009 年

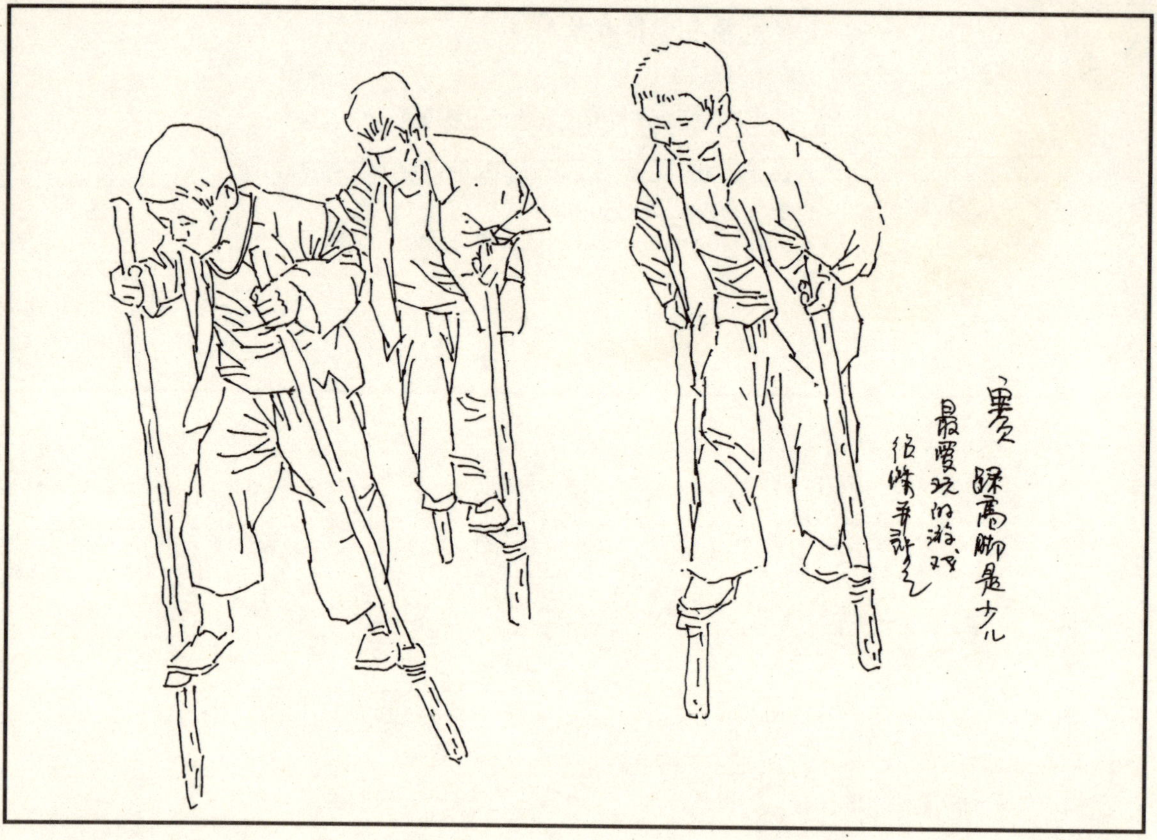

2008 年

踩高脚马

（永顺　泽家）

高脚马由两根木棍上各加绑一脚踩木构成，是湘西地区小孩子们最喜爱的传统娱乐和体育竞技运动。

Stilts

Location: Zejia, Yongshun
A traditional form of entertainment and sports in Xiangxi.

织花带

（永顺　对山）

土家族花带的制作，一切均在织造者双膝间完成。永顺县八十高龄的熊得文老人是远近闻名的编织高手。

Weaving a Belt

Location: Duishan, Yongshun
Xiong Dewen, an eighty-year-old lady, is recognized as a weaving master among the local people.

2007 年

不二门

(永顺　灵溪)

不二门是一座国家级森林公园，位于永顺县城南 1.5 千米处的猛洞河畔，以奇石、温泉、石刻为其特色。两石壁倾斜成“人”字门形，一小道穿洞而至观音古寺，取自佛教“不二法门”之意。

Bu’ermen

Location: Lingxi, Yongshun

Bu’ermen means Nonduality Gate. Bu’ermen is a national forest park which features astonishing rocks, thermal springs and stone carvings. This is also where you can worship Guanyin, the Goddess of Mercy.

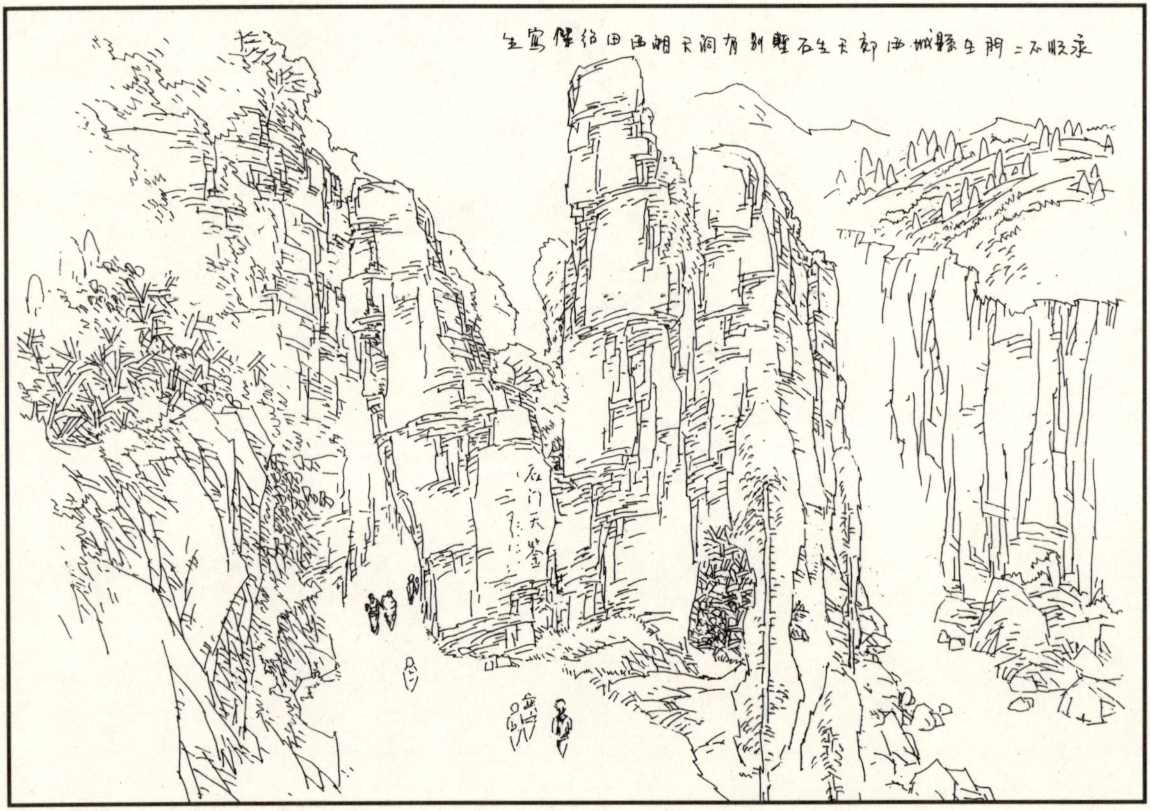

2007 年

观音庙大殿

（永顺　灵溪）

一座供奉观音，带有土家族民居特色的翘檐楼阁式寺庙殿宇。

The Grand Guanyin Temple.

Location: Lingxi, Yongshun

The Tujia building style is incorporated in this temple, which features flying eaves and tower elements.

1985 年

2007 年

观音岩

（永顺　灵溪）

观音庙修筑在一块非常像观音形状的巨石上，其石被称为观音岩。

Guanyin Rock

Location: Lingxi, Yongshun
The rock got its name from its resemblance to the figure of Guanyin.

老司城祖师殿

（永顺　麻岔）

老司城原名福石城，建于南宋绍兴五年（1135），在永顺县城东 20 千米处，为全国重点文物保护单位。自五代起至清雍正“改土归流”，一直是土司王统治溪州数百年的王城。现仅存的正殿、皇经台、玉皇阁依次沿中轴线排列。祖师殿相传为纪念鲁班显灵所建，供奉鲁班神像，是一座颇具湘西土家族特色的建筑。

Ancestral Hall of Laosicheng

Location: Macha, Yongshun
Laosicheng (the old chief's town) was built in 1135. Until 1729 it had been the capital city of Yongshun from which the local cheiftan ruled over ancient Xizhou. Ancestral Hall is a building with many outstanding characteristics of Xiangxi Tujia.

2008 年

灵溪古渡

（永顺　麻岔）

老司城下灵溪河畔的古渡口。

The Ancient Ferry of Lingxi

Location: Macha, Yongshun
The ancient ferry below Laosicheng.

2008 年

摆手舞

（永顺　双凤）

摆手舞是土家族祈祷祭祖时所跳的一种娱人娱神的群众性舞蹈。有古诗赞曰：“福石城中锦作窝，土王宫畔水生波。红灯万盏人千叠，一片缠绵摆手歌。”

The Baishou Dance

Location: Shuangfeng, Yongshun

Baishou Dance is a group dance which is part of the ancestor worship activities.

2006 年

2009年

石板老街

(永顺　王村)

王村为湘西四大名镇之一，秦汉为酉阳县治，因其为土司王的都城而得名，有“楚蜀通津”之誉。瀑布、古街、吊脚楼是王村的三绝，土家族文化和土司文化是王村的二奇。因电影《芙蓉镇》在此拍摄，故别称“芙蓉镇”。主街为一条青石板嵌成的五里长街，依地势蜿蜒伸展。

Old Stone Street

Location: Wangcun, Yongshun
The historic town , Wangcun, meaning king's village, used to be the capital when local chieftains (Tusi) ruled the area. It is also called Furong (Hibiscus) town.

老码头

（永顺　王村）

王村石板老街尽头的码头是酉水河上重要码头之一。其上通川黔，下连鄂沪。

Old Wharf

Location: Wangcun, Yongshun
The wharf in Wangcun is one of the important wharfs alongside Youshui River.

1985 年

王村大瀑布

（永顺　王村）

猛洞河风光带内的第二大瀑布，分为两级瀑布。

Wangcun Water Falls

Location: Wangcun, Yongshun
A two-step water falls.

2001 年

飞水寨

（永顺　王村）

历代土司王的避暑之地，依山傍瀑立于悬崖之上，是一组具有土家族建筑特色的建筑群。

Feishui Village

Location: Wangcun, Yongshun

Built on the cliff, this group of Tujia style buildings had been the local chieftans' summer resort for generations.

2007年

将军桥

(永顺　王村)

石桥，据说是为“溪州之战”中得胜归来的土家将军修建的。

The Jiangjun Bridge

Location: Wangcun, Yongshun
Jiangjun means General. A very old arch stone bridge.

2008年

猛洞河漂流

（永顺　抚志）

猛洞河系酉水支流，全长100千米。有“天下第一漂”之称的猛洞河漂流位于猛洞河支流司河，上起哈妮宫，下至猴儿跳，全长37千米，集奇、幽、野、趣于一体。

Rafting on Mengdong River

Location: Fuzhi, Yongshun

Mengdong River, 100 kilometers long, is a branch of Youshui River. Rafting on Mengdong River combines quietude, wildness, wonder, and delight.

2009 年

酉水河畔

(永顺　王村)

站在王村码头远眺酉水河，风光无限。

On the sanks of the Youshui River

Location: Wangcun, Yongshun
Youshui River is the main river in Xiangxi.

2001 年 11 月 28 日

落水坑瀑布

（永顺　抚志）

猛洞河漂流中所见最壮观的瀑布群。

Luoshuikeng Falls

Location: Fuzhi, Yongshun
The most spectacular waterfalls along the tour of Mengdonghe

2003 年

小溪土家山寨

（永顺　小溪）

小溪是国家自然生态保护区，为亚热带低海拔常绿阔叶原始一次生森林，是免遭第四纪冰川侵袭而幸存的天然绿色基因库，有“世界植物宝库活化石”和“天然氧吧”之誉称。

Xiaoxi Tujia Village

Location: Xiaoxi, Yongshun
Xiaoxi is the only primeval forest that escaped destruction from the impact of the fourth ice age.

2001 年

小溪吊脚楼

（永顺　小溪）

盖着杉木树皮的小溪土家族民居。

Xiaoxi Houses on Stilts

Location: Xiaoxi, Yongshun
The village house on stilts covered with the barks of China fir.

2001 年 11 月 29 日

小溪人家

（永顺　小溪）

带回廊的全木结构吊脚楼。

Homes of Xiaoxi people

Location: Xiaoxi, Yongshun
The all wooden dwellings on stilts with corridors.

2007 年

2005 年

丁家院子

（永顺　塔卧）

塔卧曾是中国土地革命时期湘鄂川黔革命根据地的中心，这里完整保存着当时红二、红六军团及中华苏维埃共和国湘鄂川黔省革命委员会旧址——丁家院子。丁家院子系典型的土家族民居建筑。

Ding-Family Courtyard

Location: Tawo, Yongshun
A typical Tujia dwelling.

2006 年

土家姑娘

（永顺　塔卧）

土家姑娘素以勤劳朴实、吃苦耐劳而著称，民间有称赞的谚语“颗砂的米，塔卧的女”。

Tujia Girls

Location: Tawo, Yongshun
Tujia girls have always been known for their purity and hardwork.

古丈

Guzhang

清道光二年（1822），建置古丈坪厅，而得今名古丈。因属苗疆要地，与凤凰、乾州、永绥三厅统称“苗疆四厅”。

Guzhang is named after Guzhangping town (part of today's Guzhang Town) which was built in this area in 1822.

栖凤湖

（古丈　罗依溪）

栖凤湖为凤滩库区人工高峡平湖。四周环以连绵起伏的高山峡谷。湖岸线曲折多变，形成许多三面临水的半岛。土家吊脚楼傍山依水而建，与湖上点点白帆相映成趣。

Qifeng Lake

Location: Luoyixi, Guzhang

The scenic artificial lake in the mountain-based valley .

2009 年

茶叶之乡

（古丈　罗依溪）

栖凤湖畔是湘西重要的茶叶产地，“古丈毛尖”名扬中外。

Tea Country

Location: Luoyixi, Guzhang
The famous tea , Guzhangmaojian is produced here.

2009 年

岩排溪

（古丈　高峰）

古丈县岩排溪与沅陵交界，距县城 80 千米，山高林密。山寨藏于深山之中，为清一色的吊脚楼。吊脚楼群依山而建，原始古朴，亦为湘西所罕见。石灰岩砌筑而成的层层梯田，伴着村落以自然随性的姿态散落于山中。此处的灌溉设施虽历经数百年风雨，依旧泽惠着后世。

Yanpaixi

Location: Gaofeng, Guzhang
Tujia settlement, houses on stilts and terraced farmland.

2009 年

岩排溪吊脚楼

（古丈　高峰）

岩排溪的吊脚楼民居，有的吊脚上饰有金瓜、绣球，有的门窗上雕有精美的纹饰图案。

Houses on stilts at Yanpaixi

Location: Gaofeng, Guzhang
The architectural decoration of houses at Yanpaixi is very exquisite.

2009年

岩排溪吊脚楼群

（古丈　高峰）

一个上规模、具特色的典型古民居建筑群，包含有三合楼、转角楼以及配有“美人靠”的吊脚楼等多种民居建筑式样。

Group of Houses on stilts at Yanpaixi

Location: Gaofeng, Guzhang

These ancient dwellings on a large scale are tasteful and unique.

2009 年

红石林奇观

（古丈　茄通）

红石林面积有 9000 多公顷，石峰星罗棋布、千姿百态，石峰色彩变化多样，为不可多得的地质奇观。每一座岩石都像一幅美妙的图画、一首优美的诗歌。

The Red Rock Forest

Location: Qietong, Guzhang

This forest of red rock covers an area of more than 9000 hectares.

2008 年

红石林的大山

（古丈　茄通）

中国唯一的红色碳酸盐岩石林。拥有着石林地貌形成演化全过程的所有地质遗迹，被称为“红石林博物馆”。

The Big Mountain of the Red Rock Forest

Location: Qietong, Guzhang
The only carbonate rock forest in China.

2002 年

背扎篓的土家姑娘

（古丈　田家洞）

土家地区山高坡陡、道路崎岖。竹背篓是土家男女均喜爱的日常工具。扎篓是竹背篓的一种。

Tujia Girl with Back-Basket

Location: Tianjiadong, Guzhang

Back-basket is a handy item popular in this mountainous area of Xiangxi.

2007 年

龙山
Longshan

龙山县位于湘西北部边陲，地处武陵山脉腹地，连荆楚而挽巴蜀，历史上称之为"湘鄂川之孔道"。清雍正七年（1729）建置。

Established in 1729, Longshan county is situated on the northwest boarder of Hu'nan Province in the hinterland of Wuling Ridge.

里耶古街

（龙山　里耶）

里耶是湘西北酉水河畔的边陲古镇，历经沧桑，有令人扼腕浩叹的历史。此处有我国考古史上发现的第一座秦代古城，所出土的 3.6 万枚秦代简牍以及古朴原始的土家族文化为世人瞩目。形成于清代初期的里耶老街，每条街道都直通河码头。

Historic Street in Liye

Location: Liye, Longshan

Liye is an ancient border town alongside the Youshui River in Xiangxi. This ancient city dating to the Qin Dynasty (221 B.C. - 206 B.C.) was the first such to be found in the history of archeological discovery. The ancient Liye streets, first built in Qing dynasty (1616-1911 A.D.) , each lead directly to the wharfs of the river.

2006 年

里耶老码头

（龙山　里耶）

酉水河岸上的吊脚木楼与水上的船只，形成了里耶古埠独特的风景线。

The Old Wharf in Liye

Location: Liye, Longshan
The wooden dwellings on stilts and the boats on the river blend into a fascinating picture.

1990 年

里耶街口

（龙山　里耶）

沿街望去，一排排翘角屋檐、封火墙的吊脚木楼建筑，十分壮观。

Street view in Liye

Location: Liye, Longshan

The spectacular view of the wooden dwellings on stilts along the Liye street.

2009 年

织锦姑娘

（龙山　苗儿滩）

土家织锦是首批国家非物质文化遗产项目之一。土家姑娘刘艳和张水英是织锦佼佼者，为“第一届中国优秀织锦工艺传承人”。

Weaving Girls

Location: Miaoertan, Longshan

Tujia Weaving Craft was among the first among to be listed the Intangible Cultural Heritage of China.

2006 年

隆头码头

（龙山　隆头）

隆头是古酉水河上有名的老码头，这里曾商贾云集，十分繁华。古街依山顺势，土家民居与明清商埠建筑交相晖映。从古码头、古石板街的斑驳印痕，依稀能想像隆头古镇当年的辉煌。

Longtou Wharf

Location: Longtou, Longshan
A well-known old wharf at Youshui River.

2005 年

2005年

隆头古街巷

（龙山　隆头）

拾级而上，青色的石屋和黑色的木楼，错落有致。

Historic Street in Longtou

Location: Longtou, Longshan
The dark-blue stone huts and black wooden buildings draw a picturesque skyline with their casual arrangement.

望月

（龙山　洗车河）

土家族的小孩满月，父母两家的亲戚好友都要来庆贺，称“望月”，也称“粥米酒”。

Wangyue

Location: Xichehe, Longshan

Wangyue is a tradition where friends and relatives come to celebrate when a baby turns one month old.

2006 年

洗车河古镇

（龙山　洗车河）

洗车河又称香溪，是捞车河上游的支流。这一带桂馥兰芳，蓼红蓝白，为土家族文化保留最为完好的原生态区域之一。洗车河镇坐落于洗车河与猛西河汇合处，一座建于乾隆四十五年（1780）的风雨桥横跨洗车河上。这座风雨桥与两河沿岸的一片片乌瓦吊脚楼是洗车河镇的标志性建筑。

Xichehe Ancient Town

Location: Xichehe, Longshan
The original Tujia culture is best preserved in Xichehe region.
Xichehe Town is located at the convergence of Xichehe River and Mengxihe River. The Wind-rain Bridge built in 1780 and the houses on stilts alongside the Xichehe streets are the symbols here.

2006 年

洗车河石拱桥

（龙山　洗车河）

洗车河石拱桥在两河交汇之处，石拱桥、吊脚楼交相辉映，为洗车河景观一绝。

The Stone Arch Bridge in Xichehe

Location: Xichehe, Longshan

The stone arch bridge in Xichehe is located at the meeting place of the two rivers. The bridge and the houses on stilts over the rivers mark the unique landscape of this town.

2009 年

土家织锦老艺人

（龙山　苗儿滩）

捞车河流域是土家织锦“中国工艺美术大师”叶玉翠的故里，织锦至今仍是这一带土家妇女的当家手艺。

The Old Weaver

Location: Miaoertan, Longshan
Weaving remains the most valued craft of Tujia women.

2009年

坡脚杨家寨

（龙山　坡脚）

坡脚是典型的土家族聚居区，交通闭塞。这里是中国土家族的语言、习俗保留最为完好的地方，有“中国土家原生态民俗博物馆”之称。

Yangjia Village in Pojiao

Location: Pojiao, Longshan
Tujia language and traditions are best preserved in Pojiao, which area is known as "the museum of original Tujia culture of China"

1991 年

背亲出嫁

（龙山　坡脚）

在湘西土家族的婚姻习俗中，新娘出嫁是不能自己走上花轿的，必须由新娘的亲兄弟或堂、表兄弟背送上花轿，亦称“背亲”，以求吉祥。

Carry to “Give Away"

Location: Pojiao, Longshan
A wedding tradition of Xiangxi Tujia people.

2005 年

花垣

Huayuan

花垣，原为明朝保靖宣慰司彭氏宴游的花园，后筑城垣，年久而得名花垣。清嘉庆三年（1798）建置，名永绥县，1952 年更名花垣县。

Huayuan used to be the garden of Peng, a chieftain (Tusi) in the Ming Dynasty (1368—1644 A.D.). Walls enclosing the garden were built afterward.

边城古渡口

（花垣　茶峒）

茶峒位于湘渝黔三省市交界处，是沈从文先生笔下《边城》的原型，有“三峰林楚蜀，一山阁川黔，一脚踏三省”之称。

Historic Ferry in Biancheng

Location: Chadong, Huayuan
The historic town served as the model for Shen Congwen's novel, Biancheng.

2008 年

茶峒老街

（花垣　茶峒）

茶峒河边的老街，古色古香。土家吊脚楼与赣式商铺建筑的完美结合，耐人寻味。

Old Street in Chatong

Location: Chadong, Huayuan

A good collection of Tujia houses on stilts and the Gan (Jiangxi Province) style of architecture.

2008 年

古苗河

（花垣　花垣）

古苗河在花垣县城的近郊，相传为苗族远古先祖蚩尤为根治水患所开，故又称蚩尤河。

The Historic Miaohe River

Location: Huayuan, Huayuan
According to legend, Chiyou. the ancestor of the Miao people dug this river to relieve floods, thus, the river also called the Chiyou River.

2002 年 10 月

古苗河边老头峰

(花垣　花垣)

古苗河多为岩溶地貌，险奇秀美，是寻幽的好去处。老头峰为一形似老人头的山峰。

Old-man Peak at Miaohe River

Location: Huayuan, Huayuan
The ancient Miaohe area is mainly karst landform. Old-man peak was so called because its peak resembled an old man's head.

1999 年

泸溪

Luxi

唐武德二年（619），将军董珍建卢溪县，武水出口一段被称为卢水，河北有卢山，因此而得县名。清顺治六年（1649），改为泸溪县。

Established in 619 A.D., Luxi County was named after the Lu River and the Lu Mountain north of the river.

神秘的箱子岩

（泸溪　白沙）

沈从文笔下的箱子岩悬棺遗址位于泸溪境内的沅水流域。神秘的悬棺系湘西古代先民的一种丧葬习俗，也称崖墓葬，其遗址在沅水、酉水两岸的悬崖峭壁上多处可见。

Site of Suspended Coffins on the Xiangzi Rock

Location: Baisha, Luxi

Laying bodies in a suspended coffin was a tradition of ancient native people.

2008 年

2008 年

辛女岩

（泸溪　白沙）

辛女岩位于泸溪。据考："辛女岩、邑西三十里，危峰高耸，有石屹立如人，相传高辛氏之女于此化为石。"泸溪是中国盘瓠文化的发源地，辛女是盘瓠的妻子，一位美丽善良的公主。

Xinnü Rock

Location: Baisha, Luxi

Xinnü was the wife of Panhu, a dog from ancient local mythology. The Xinnü Rock lies in Luxi where the Panhu civilization originated.

保靖

Baojing

战国始有建置，为迁陵侯。西汉高祖五年（前 202）建立迁陵县。新莽改迁陆县，东汉复迁陵，三国、西晋、东晋因之。南北朝时期，齐改零陵县，梁复迁陵县。隋入大乡县。唐改三亭县、洛浦县，唐末复三亭县。五代为保静州，保靖军民安抚司。明为军民宣慰司。

清雍正五年（1727）“改土归流”，七年（1729）取“保持地方安定”之意建保靖县。

Established during the Warring States period, in 202 BC as Qianling County, it was renamed. Baojing County in 1729,meaning "maintain stability" .

拔茅寨

（保靖　拔茅）

拔茅寨位于保靖县城西北 30 千米的酉水南岸，邻接土家族圣地——八部大王庙遗址和酉水崖墓群。古寨古风，奇特多姿，被南来北往的艺术家誉为土家族“酉水河上第一寨”。

Bamao Village

Location: Bamao, Baojing

Because Miscanthus Floridulus, which is pronounced "bamao" in Chinese grows all over the mountain, the village is so called. The village was built against the mountain and along the Youshui River, with a beautiful view and fertile land.The Tujia historic village is acclaimed as the First Village on Youshui River.

1990 年

拔茅寨老街

（保靖　拔茅）

拔茅寨老街依山就势，青石台阶蜿蜒而上，吊脚木楼鳞次栉比。古寨深巷，记述着一个个古老而动听的故事。

Old Streets in Bamao Village

Location: Bamao, Baojing
The old streets of Bamao village were built against the mountain, with the stone stair zigzagging up to the top, dotted with houses on stilts.

1990年

1990 年

拔茅吊脚楼

（保靖　拔茅）

一座石桥将山两边的村寨连成一体，吊脚楼依山就势，自然天成。

Bamao Dwellings on Stilts

Location: Bamao, Baojing
A stone bridge links the two villages on the mountain sides.

土家族老人

（保靖　拔茅）

头缠青丝布帕、身着对胸便服，是土家族男性的传统服饰。

An Old Tujia Man

Location: Bamao, Baojing
An old Tujia man in black hoad cloth and a casual jacket.

1998 年

八部大王庙遗址——首八峒

(保靖　拔茅)

首八峒，又名水扒峒。此处有湘西唯一一处纪念土家族先祖的八部大王庙遗址。庙前有碑铭一块，刻有联云：“勋猷垂筒篇驰封八部，灵爽式斯土血食千秋”。

Shoubadong

Location: Bamao, Baojing

The site of Babu King Temple, the only temple in Xiangxi dedicated to the Tujia people's ancestors.

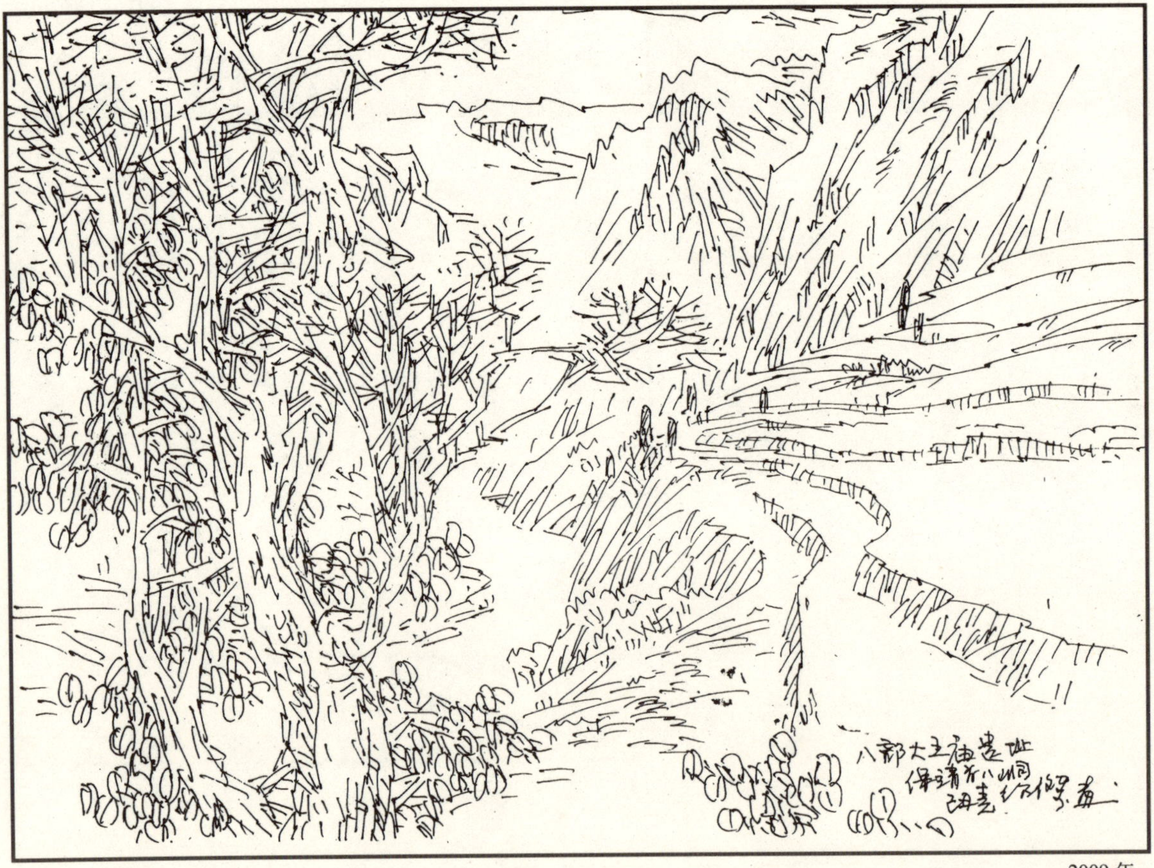

2009 年

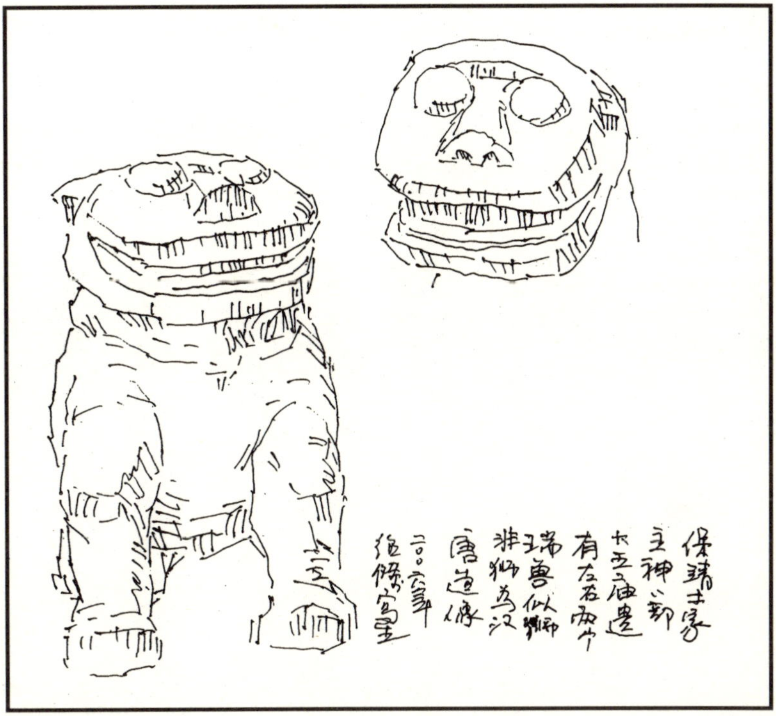

2006 年

瑞兽

（保靖　拔茅）

八部大王庙遗址残存的瑞兽，左右一对，似狮非狮。

Stone Beasts

Location: Bamao, Baojing

These stone carvings of beasts lie in the Babu King Temple ruins.

酉水船歌

（保靖　拔茅）

酉水河古属五溪的酉溪，是沅水最大的一条支流，流经湘西北土家族集聚的龙山、保靖、永顺、古丈四县，被誉为湘西土家族的母亲河。船工拉纤时的呐喊声雄浑而悲凉，其歌词反映了酉水沿岸的民俗风情和船工的艰辛。

Youshui Boat Songs

Location: Bamao, Baojing

The songs chanted by the boat trackers, have haunting lyrics revealing the customs of the local people at Youshuihe River.

1984 年

酉水河边人家

（保靖　拔茅）

住在酉水河边的吊脚楼的人们，乌篷船是出行的主要交通工具。

Life on Youshui River

Location: Bamao, Baojing
The wupeng (black roofed) boat is the main means of transportation of the people living along the river.

1990 年

张家界

Zhangjiajie

张家界是中国第一座国家森林公园。这里属石英砂岩峰林地貌，孤峰簇簇，溪水潺潺，鸟语花香，森林覆盖率高达 97%。1992 年，由张家界国家森林公园、索溪峪风景区、天子山风景区三大景区构成的武陵源自然风景区被联合国教科文组织列入《世界自然遗产名录》。

Zhangjiajie is the first national forest park in China and was listed by UNESCO as a World Natural Heritage Site in 1992.

〔张家界〕

（武陵源　张家界国家森林公园）

相传汉代名相张良隐居于此而得名。这里石峰林立、风景优美。

Zhangjiajie

Location: Zhangjiajie National Forest Park, Wulingyuan
Zhangjiajie got its name due to the fact that Zhang Liang, the famous official of Han Dynasty (221 B.C. - 220 A. D.), went into seclusion here.

2006 年

2009 年

金鞭溪

（武陵源　张家界国家森林公园）

金鞭溪因流经金鞭岩而得名，全长 5.7 千米，穿行于绝壁奇峰之间，溪谷有繁茂的植被，溪水四季清澈，被誉为“世界上最美丽的峡谷之一”。

Jinbian Stream

Location: Zhangjiajie National Forest Park, Wulingyuan
Jinbian means Golden Whip.
So called because it passes the Golden Whip Rock. With the length of 5700 meters, it has been called one of the most beautiful canyons in the world.

自生桥

（武陵源　天子山）

自生桥又名仙人桥，横跨于两座高耸入云的石峰之间，长约26米，宽不足2米，厚约1.5-2.7米。

The Zisheng Bridge

Location: Tianzi Mountain, Wulingyuan

Zisheng means Self-born. The Zisheng Bridge is also called Xianren Bridge. The natural bridge links two tall stone peaks. It is about 26 meters long, less than 2 meters thick, and about 1.5 to 2.7 meters wide.

2009年

空中田园

（武陵源　天子山）

空中田园是位于张家界天子山老屋场小景区的中间台地，与袁家界隔谷相望。小块台地悬于半空，一面是群峰高耸，余则为陡崖险谷。台地上梯田层层，尽种水稻。台地上有世代居住的土家人十几户，青墙黑瓦、绿树斜阳、菜畦青青、炊烟袅袅，如人间仙境。

Farmland in the Sky

Location: Tianzi Mountain, Wulingyuan

This refers to the farmland and village in the high land of Tianzi mountain in Zhangjiajie.

2009 年

袁家界

（武陵源　天子山）

袁家界地处张家界世界自然遗产的核心，以雄、奇、险、峻著称。

Yuanjiajie

Location: Tianzi Mountain, Wulingyuan
Situated in the center of Zhangjiajie, Yuanjiajie is famous for its majestic, imposing, views of sheer cliffs.

2009 年

后花园（一）

（武陵源　天子山）

后花园是袁家界的重点景区，位于袁家界中坪与下坪交接处，是一处藏而不露的景观。游人在崖间丛林中穿行，突然被一面石壁挡住。却见绝壁拐弯处，有一满月状白石洞。穿洞而过，眼前突现数十座奇峰耸立于墨绿深涧之中。俯瞰山下溪谷，景象万千。

Back Garden (1)

Location: Tianzi Mountain, Wulingyuan
Back Garden is the most important attraction of Yuanjiajie.

2010年

后花园（二）

（武陵源　天子山）

Back Garden (2)

Location: Tianzi Mountain, Wulingyuan

2010 年

后花园（三）

（武陵源　天子山）

Back Garden (3)

Location: Tianzi Mountain, Wulingyuan

2010 年

后花园（四）

（武陵源　天子山）

Back Garden (4)

Location: Tianzi Mountain, Wulingyuan

2010 年

2010年

回音壁

（武陵源　天子山）

回音壁是天子山景区一片林立的石峰。面对群山高喊一声，回声似千军万马奔腾。

The Echo Wall

Location: Tianzi Mountain, Wulingyuan

It refers to the stone forest in Tianzi Mountain. A single yell is answered by the roar of an army of thousands.

杨家寨天波府

（武陵源　天子山）

杨家寨天波府是一座独立的山峰，靠人工修建的扶梯才能上去。杨家寨以相传北宋杨家将后裔隐居在此而得名。因其僻处乡野、自然朴实，被称为“冒险家的乐园”。

Tianpo Palace in Yangjiazhai (Yang Family Village)

Location: Tianzi Mountain, Wulingyuan

The Tianpo Palace in Yangjiazhai is located at a lone peak. It could be reached only by the man-made stairway. It was named after the famous family of warriors from the North Song Dynasty (960-1127A.D.), whose descendants settled here after their defeat.

2010年

杨家寨将军椅

（武陵源　天子山）

将军椅天生形似座椅，民间传说是当年杨令公的帅座。

The General's Chair

Location: Tianzi Mountain, Wulingyuan
A chair-shaped peak.

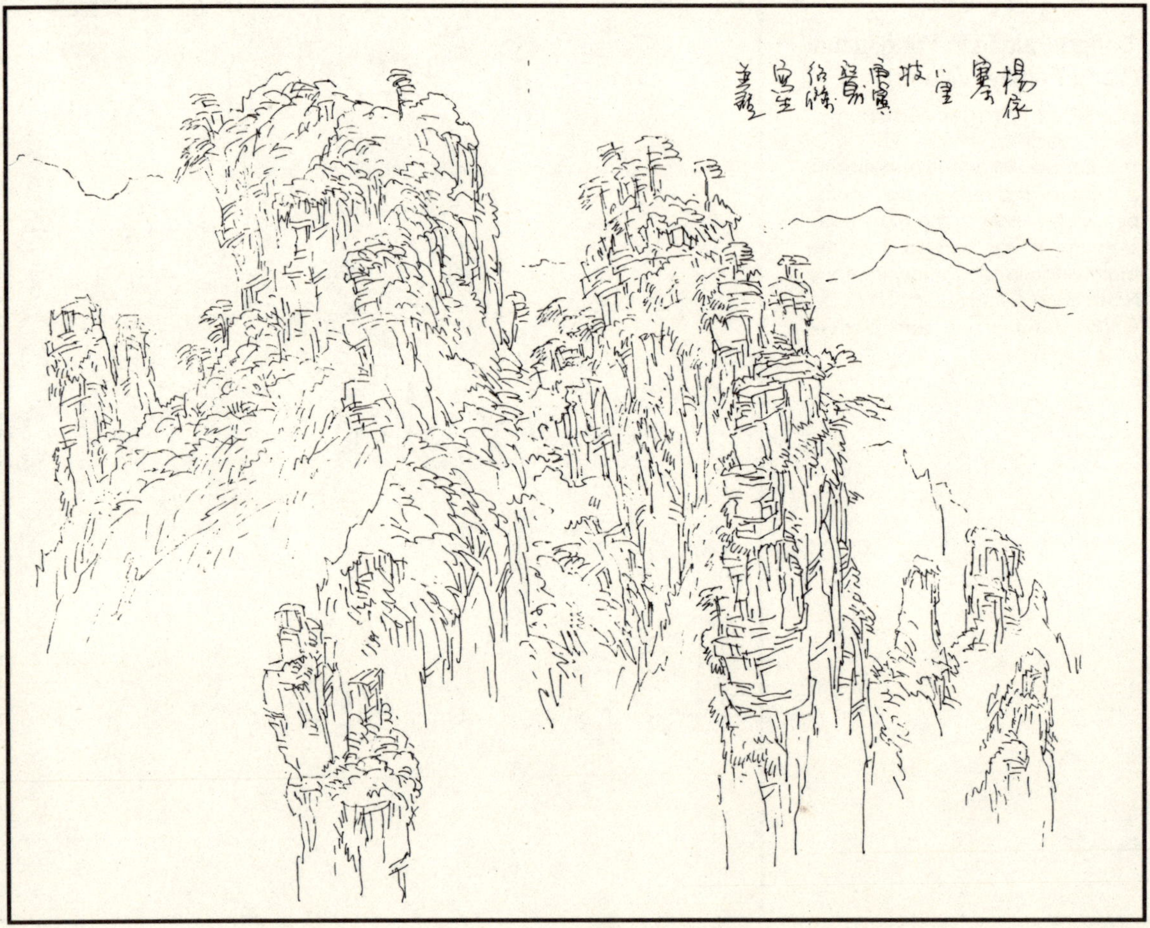

2010 年

乌龙寨

（武陵源　天子山）

乌龙寨位于杨家寨的半山腰，原名“黑龙寨”。地处偏远，关隘险绝，四面悬崖，仅有一条道上下，地势险要，所谓“一夫当关，万夫莫开”。几间吊脚木楼，原始而古朴。

Wulong Village

Location: Tianzi Mountain, Wulingyuan

A village half way up to Yangjiazhai. The few wooden houses on stilts are quite old and simple.

2010年

水绕四门

（武陵源　索溪峪）

因有三条溪水，分别从西、北、南三面峡谷流出，然后相汇合流，注入索溪，故称水绕四门。

Shuiraosimen

Location: Suoxiyu, Wulingyuan
Streams from three different valleys join into a river.

2001 年

2008 年

宝峰湖

（武陵源　索溪峪）

宝峰湖风景区集山水于一体，融民俗风情于一身，尤以奇秀的高峡平湖、“飞流直下三千尺”的宝峰飞瀑、神秘的深山古寺闻名。以其秀丽的湖光水色与幽野的洞天情趣成为武陵源水景风光的代表。

Baofeng Lake

Location: Suoxiyu, Wulingyuan

A lake high up in the mountains. With the beautiful lake view and the mysterious cave scenes, it has become one of the biggest attractions of Wuling waters.

2007年

宝峰飞瀑

（武陵源　索溪峪）

宝峰桥边山腰上飞流而下的瀑布。先直泻而下，后顺坡漫洒于桥下池中。两水池相叠，波光荧荧。

Baofeng Falls: Falling straight from the Heavens.

Location: Suoxiyu, Wulingyuan
The falls rushing down from the waist of mountain near Baofeng bridge. It seems to fall straight from the heavens.

2004 年

天门山

（永定　大坪）

天门山古称嵩梁山，亦叫云梦山，坐落在张家界市区近郊，素以佛教闻名遐迩。山势挺拔，天门洞洞穿山体，形成天门奇观。三国吴永安六年 (263)，吴王改武陵郡为天门郡，始得其名。

Tianmen Mountain

Location: Daping, Yongding
The rock has been eroded to form this natural wonder.

罗塔坪将军岩

（永定　罗塔坪）

罗塔坪位于张家界之西，为石英砂岩峰林地貌。这里地势相对开阔，在奇峰断崖之间，梯田层层，吊脚楼时隐时现。

The General's Rock on Luotaping

Location: Luotaping, Yongding
Luotanping area features sandstone peak forest landform.

1988 年

风车车谷

（永定　四都坪）

风车是湘西地区的一种农具。晒谷场上，人们用风车车谷，分出谷粒和杂草。

Winnow

Location: Siduping, Yongding
Winnows are used for farming in Xiangxi Region.

2006年

洪家关贺龙桥

（桑植　洪家关）

洪家关距桑植县城15千米，是贺龙元帅的故乡。因明太祖在此设征税关卡而得名。贺龙桥原名永安桥，是贺龙曾祖父贺廷宰首倡修建的。它是一座由石墩、木梁、檐廊构成的风雨桥。这座桥因人祸水患，屡遭厄运。1952年重建后，命名为“贺龙桥”。

He Long Bridge in Hongjiaguan

Location: Hongjiaguan, Sangzhi

Hongjiaguan is the hometown of General He Long (1896 -1969 A.D.) . It is a covered bridge with stone seats, wooden beams and shaded corridors.

2008年

五道水

(桑植　五道水)

五道水位于桑植县境内湘鄂边界，是湖南省四大水系之一澧水的源头，有名的“七眼泉”即在此。五道水森林茂密，民风纯朴，是探险寻幽的好去处。

Wudaoshui

Location: Wudaoshui, Sangzhi
Wudaoshui is the beginning of Lishui River which is one of the four main rivers of Hu'nan Province.

1990 年

五雷山

（慈利　广福桥）

五雷山又名大维山，位于慈利县城东北15千米处，为中国南方规模宏伟的道教圣地之一，有中国“南武当”之誉称，始于唐，鼎盛于明清，有36宫、72殿、48寨。

Wulei Mountain

Location: Guangfuqiao, Cili
Wulei Mountain has become one of the greatest Daoist holy places in south China due to its substantial shrines.

2008年